WOMAN IN APARTMENT

ams press
new york

DEDICATION

To My Mother and the Memory of My Father

WOMAN
IN APARTMENT

CYNTHIA PICKARD

NEW POETRY SERIES

ALAN SWALLOW, *Denver*

Library of Congress Cataloging in Publication Data

Pickard, Cynthia.
    Woman in apartment.

    Reprint of the 1957 ed. published by A. Swallow, Denver,
in series: The New poetry series.
    I. Title.
[PS3531.I257W6   1975]   811'.5'4   72-179817
ISBN 0-404-56017-2
        0-404-56000-8 (SET)

The New Poetry Series

Reprinted by arrangement with
The Swallow Press Inc.
Copyright © 1957 by Cynthia Pickard
First AMS edition published in 1975
AMS Press Inc. 56 E. 13th St.
New York, N.Y. 10003

Manufactured in the USA

811.54
PiC

CONTENTS

AFFECTIONS:

A Group of Experimental Sonnets

WOMAN IN APARTMENT

I sat in my kitchen and longed at the linoleum,
Figured at the curves and what the colors meant
And the enamel everywhere present
And thought of the day, that you were there, and
    welcome.

And then I heard from the bordered bedroom some
Singing—oh just from the radio, the prurient
Tune; I thought of the night, innocent
Of you. And then from the flowery parlor it came:

Quiet (parlors are built to be that way)
Acceptance of guests that only just stopped by
Expecting nothing from you but a smile and coffee
And wasn't the weather capricious and coy today?
I thought, I can do it, can serve them; I thought, I
Have still my armored kitchen for revelry.

CAMEO

Lying with the trinkets in my glitter chest
This apart—cameo engraved in bone.
Or is it, as I suspect, precious stone?
I have sometimes thought of having it appraised.
But I need no jeweller, magnificent eye upraised,
Telling me value of the image I own.
I know it's unique when I pin it on
And finger the high-relief carving. *O handsomest.*

Not for me to be like one woman
Who wore pink pink pink and she wore pink
Until once we felt estranged when she dolled in white.
So, since only the blind would see this no omen,
I wear it on the occasional day, but think:
I have the cameo decorating my night.

FLOWERED TRIP

I've lugged this box from the florist's till one finger
Is numb of the burden bought; but I chose with care
And walk quickly in fragrance, knowing that there
Are seldom roots from the stem of any cut flower.
Yet roots alone to live on would be error.
They have food storage but for the better air
That's perfumed all a person could possibly bear
Roots are generally thought to be inferior.

Home, I will arrange the roses in a vase
And gaze at them and gaze a little time
Then when the petals begin their dark turning
I will, if I have any regard for the place
Where I must live and others look, toss them
Out to where death can do a carrying.

BIRD DREAM

I dreamed that a once-my-starling, once-my-love,
Sat by, but with a still bill. And then his eyes
Preened sentimentally, sang something like sighs;
And then his eyes lifted a wing that was wanting to give
The old touch: much. And all that he could have
Not seen, yes seen but as do sparrows
He saw; and then his eyes flew fighting at these:
"Snakes in this garden, go dog you a dove!"

Now what hope could a dream like that have?
Only a morning set for finance's measure
Starting at the squawk of *Once* O but then
Out of the hour that *Now* is to the hatched relief
That seeing him and his eyes for one flutter
Again with a difference might be good again.

NOTHING IS LOST

No not lost, even in deprivation.
Let me catalog a little: a scholar
With one good shirt and enough hard soap went far;
She with no lover birthed a love religion;
A black boy, knowing necessarily the food rich in
Being, made much of peanuts till they do endure.
I could go on if you need convincing or
Have not seen yourself . . . remember the night on

Which you thought it difficult even a personal
Fault that an angel who had called had not found you
And you turned on all the lights so he couldn't go
    wrong.
Morning came but he did not, and all
Was over between you two; this you knew
And quit staying home. Evenings you went dancing.

LIGHT ON THE WATER

The river is muddy? In the main, utility?
You see it as it is, in the realistic shade?
Granted it works for the roots, even makes a trade
For some of the richness just to flush it on to the sea.

The river is for drowning you and me?
Yes, it's deep, and where's the whirlpool hid?
I'll wait to argue death with the experienced
But this is quick, over at the count of three.

The sun is raining on the wrinkles, and they don't die.
That slow flow is alive on down your way.
Why, it's Christmas! It's the Fourth of July!
Sparklers right out of heaven celebrate me.
(Blackbird, I know your noisiness. Fly, fly.
I'll have only the silent silver today.)

THE SLAP

I should've remembered, but primer ways aren't mental
And I was happy at a neighbor's desk though the
Command was home. Impropriety
But I had no sin in mind when so I fell:
It was by accident I landed in hell.
O she spread, bigger than the Bad Man could be,
Giant on fire at the eyes, and they on me.
Then the blow from a hand that had pretended gentle.

Through the raw recess, through a day and a day and
    a day
I thought no Santa Claus, I thought no elf,
But only the huge hand, still on me, and the way
Of suddenness, and dug a fisted self
Into a pocket, little on the high, on the high
Shame that I had loved her, that I was I.

HALLOWE'EN

One girl was a witch as soon as the sun was down.
Goblins and ghouls that burnt-corked at the night
Stalked the street, and we saw many a sight
We had never but in nightmares met downtown.

Now midnight melts to a skeleton of groan
—Hour when all black cats are in their right—
And whatever moon was there is so blighted
That only an owl will know the dark deed done.

What at my doorstep? Ah, bundles from hell,
Wrapped up in the winding sheets of fright.
Look at the Lucifer and listen to him *ooooo*.
. . . . Hallow him into the light. Is his flesh real?
Or is he acting the villain for some sweet,
Satyr shy at his take and thanking you?

PRIMARY

The text says that nothing in itself has color
But the jagged prism has it, and something in your
Own brown sees blue. And so the censure
Of the sky, if you don't look, must be paler.

The peacock shines at the zoo. Stick him in the cellar;
Listen to the razzle-dazzle throat. The lure
Is gone. But the natural darkness will endear
Phosphorescent foam to a night sailor.

It's strange to think that the pigment of this skin
Has not the Renoir shade, stranger to call
It flesh. What eyes are behind, what within
The thinking fingers, five black bars of a jail?
Who sees your pride at the mirror brushing sheen
Into the waves of that that you name your soul?

ELEMENTS

Not to spoil the child, spare him you
And be Moses with a sudden rod. The water
You part is all attached, O but better
Break the Red umbilical Sea in two.

Your neighbor and you are old strangers. Who
Is in the yard at night, a dancing satyr,
Playing on a jews-harp? He'll likely catch you later
But put up snow palings, or pretend to.

Away now. Away from mother and all.
Your sister is your brother but neither is
In want of a waterfall unless you charge
The clouds: no injury. Only unseal
To the lover. He will grow in rain like this,
Grow at the roots, grow at the greener edge.

APPROACH TO THE BEES

I come among you, fellow alert, fellow
Lookers of clover over. Could I call you brothers
And be bland about sex? Or are you sirs
And ladies? or just so-so? Let it go . . . . though
I come among you not so neutral nor so
Negatively armed, with nothing like your stingers,
But in gloves and veil and shyness and no armor for
     stares
I come, perhaps you call it to plunder. Oh

I would not rob you really but only take
From the nectared surplus some proportionate
Unstrained sweet to breakfast me till May.
And that part of your unimpassioned attic
You will refill, every section of it,
And give it again, or such as you give it today.

WE LIKE TO THINK OF LOVE

We like to think of love as all-consuming.
Great lovers in every good story since Eden
Have maddened or died or given up a garden,
One promising much, for only the tasting
Of sweet apple lips otherwise wasting,
And they were never sorry, whether bar-laden
Or grounded for all time or chased with the maiden
To whatever non-paradise they had coming.

But do you not think the stories ought to tell
Of one who loved, but sanely, and sanity led him
Away; one, alive, stayed so, long
Past story-telling time, and dozed; another I'll
Add—or would, but gardens do take time.
We like to think of love as all-consuming.

MODERNE

This foot was a fin that had to fight off the water;
The arms stuck out with the chin in an ape challenge;
These eyes were Neanderthal slits, strange
To the four-footed, deadlier than dear.

Those days were doggerel, oh they were
Crude courage. No theoretical tinge;
After all, to fight . . . when one could arrange
Hieroglyphics and you into convenient matter.

I have made delicate progress in each millennium
To this Haviland mind, precious part
—And mind you, I shall not be degenerate.
From gulped water to sipped wine, I've come
To the rare air, and I stethoscope my heart
Not to outclimb myself for a slight summit.

POET

When you were ten, a tomboy, up in a maple,
You'd wave a wooden gun at the passers-by
And holler Halt. Seldom a robbed sigh:
They were adult and going downtown to amble.
Some are now part of the solemn rubble
At the village edge, halted by One high
In His maple, who perhaps didn't cry
What He did like a raucous kid, but was humble.

Your own tone is different from out of the tree
But if holy, and if holy, your tempered shock
It still is not the call of the calliope
(Come COME where the people are, come COME to
    the park)
And your effect in the whole activity
Seems that of a robin rubbing its head on a rock.

THE AFFECTIONATE SEAMSTRESS

Watch me take this ripped remnant of loving
And sew it into the Raggedy Ann that
I hugged as a child but after a while discarded.
I could never bear to keep a dead doll long.
Better a curious cat than a cold darling;
Better enigma than the sweetheart lips it had;
Active unintelligence—open, shut—
Beats black stitched eyes that, kissed, do nothing.

Come, I'll try you. Already the cloth shapes;
Here's some old yarn I happened to have.
Now you are stuffed and certain and sweet and I take
No kisses but give them, and smear your polite lips.
I call to No-Ears: *Hi, Eyes!* . . . . Oh, enough.
I give this guy to the indifferent attic.

JUNO ABOUT IO

Day closed with a cloud and it noon. Your evening is
Early and it is for sleep. O after her
Who has preened her youth at him till he would
    impander
The light, so ruffed his divine manliness.

Again my Olympian bed, soft as this
Morning's hope was still soft, swapped for a river
Bank, hard as experience. He has smiled his scepter
Smile and lo! the king's had a lion-size kiss.

When you hate one person you need to turn on two
And so with my hands, each with an itch, I
Held him, kneeling remorse, and I made her moo:
I got at a naked nerve with an intelligent fly.
And I'll continue. The heifer is stuck with a sting
Until she bawls like a bull and sounds my suffering.

SUNDAY CANARY

Why, this is no boarding house no though they bring
Sustenance—cabbage, cabbage a pun!
But over it, an aria. Why this redemption
That comes from a corner, from a yellow bird, from
    hanging?

Maybe it's the sunlight makes him sing the thing
Original and make a metonomy of the sun
Or he took up the coop cross and he has done
With what he surely hoped were wings for flying.

But whatever the cause, that canary there
Hasn't hunger for anything less than this:
The seeds of more psalms and the font flower.
And we are the free out in the dining air
Who pitch into the word—fork and prowess—
And crunch crunch on, eyeing the other.

AFFECTIONS

No stint all summer in the gradation of green;
We were surrounded, taken, hands up up.
You and I had stretched in the grass to top
All brag of brown, like ingots shining in
The sun but melting down to the shrubs and fern,
The million near enough to know, whose sap
Was, with us, in the great season's grip
Like the garden there, the corn and the bulging bean.

Green! . . . . No, you can bedevil pride
With praise. Not even the deserving God would have
You fanatic. And so, and with no song, there appeared
At the right a redbird, of such beauty I'd have tried
To say but see one, or see one again, for to save
Me, I could not tell you; but I cared.

TO YOU IN THE DISTANCE

What if you in the distance heard a high-low,
A singing, and nobody and no bird near?
Why, you'd whirl round, possibly even swear,
Not being St. Francis—any You I know.
You'd wonder if your sense felt it had to
Have a change and took to the atmosphere
And then you'd shrug at that no longer there,
At no-mouth airs and such la-de-da.

And then if it came again, a cloud alive,
Or as if a radio were hooked in, high,
With the volume knob, mind you, half-way to Off
—You'd have to believe in magic or an intuitive
Tower sending a wave from where, here, I
Come to you, and we meet in the music's clef.

SUBJECT OF SERMON: GOLF

Golf is not what makes the globe go round;
A round of golf is not around the world;
That on the green is not finely unfurled
And it is not really music, the sweet snapped sound.
No birdie will fly you over golden land—
Not even an eagle—to the Gate, prettily pearled,
Nor is a bogey bad enough to have snarled
You home, reformed, saved from the trapper sand.

But it is something, Sister, it is something
To so go for the control of a little ball
The big one can roll on as it is, undisciplined
By you in the fairway, Sister, Brother, sing
Out Fore for a slice of heaven or a hook at hell.
Come up to the cup, come for a chaliced end.

RAINY-DAY GRILL

The owners speak some in a boiled-egg tongue
And then in a loved lingo that's foamier.
There are more hot dogs heated and onioned here
Than all over town succulent slabs of T-bone.

I order on on, for the wrinkling rain has run
Me to this umbrella, but there is a tear of fear
In my unshrunken suit and I have hunger
For a cloth napkin served in a monotone.

A toothless neighbor sets up a tangy joke
And grins me Come to a close, wicked cavern,
Grins me more invited than the menfolk.
O I'll go back to the cool click of porcelain.
I'll turn me out into the street and soak
All odor off in the antiseptic rain.

NOVEMBER TREE

Winter would seem a strange time to go nudist.
That delicate maple really needs a scarf, and the oak,
Though muscular, must feel the chill with no cloak.
I grant him his great endowment as the brawniest
Of them all—it was his supple strength that first
Oggled my eye and I thought O. But the intake
Ended and I almost snickered: Brothers, look,
He is drunk in the wind, naked! I might have been
    cursed.

Do not, like Ham of old, deride your parent,
Either father or mother this Earth, or her own oak
Sibling she'd keep in April collar and jabot
If she could do so. Indeed, he may be indignant
At coddling that he stands stripped, flexing his talk:
How d' yuh like that trunk, these arms out so?

IDENTITY

The owl, the same old question from the would-be
    wise.
Has nobody told him that Oedipus is dead,
His body hidden, and the riddle: What dust bed,
Blown with the pollen, stings our present eyes?

The Socratic way is easy, where the query lies,
But the answer . . . the flux of the formula attempted
With only an X the same until it is said.
(And the plume plucked from the bird of paradise.)

Come with me to Iceland just for a minute,
Just long enough to store a sweetness there;
You must have something you would like to save.
Then we'll step to the desert, to the sage scent,
And watch the sun flare up in the dirt, where
A cold ghost or a wind could shiver a grave.

PORTRAIT OF A GIRL IN BLUE

"What's about blue that it is different?"
She asked at lunch, worrying the world of query.
"We eat no blue; this plum is purple really.
Man does not live by blue." She nodded assent
To herself. "And in the race of skin it is absent:
There's the red glow and yellow but not the primary
All, though white and black for intensity.
Much could be made of man with an added tint."

And she looked up at the sky and out at the iris
And over the birds that are blue. "I wonder if
It is some favorite with Him which He has
Reserved for the nearest right . . . or He may have
Just changed to conservative." Her gray-green eyes
Grew near to blue, and she looked very wise.

SONNETS ON THE WORD

DANIEL AND DARIUS

Then the men that were envious said to Darius,
"King, live forever. Our prayers are to thee;
If this is right, say it in a decree."
They dangled the bait into his pride's paws.

Then they were back. "One has you ungenerous:
Daniel petitions another majesty
He calls a god." From the pit of his entreaty
Darius heard the creak, heard the den doors close.

Pulling apart from the awful claws of night
He came calling, "Daniel!" to the lions' den.
He twisted his torn hands and made a shape of prayer;
He stood in the blood of himself from a brute bite
And cried, "Did the One God save you, then?"
And Daniel smiled. "O king, live forever."

PETER

Troubling to see. Even He on the water—
Or what specter at a storm?—quieted
Us none. But the man had a voice and when he said
Be not afraid, his eyes added, *Peter.*

I gently gravely cradled away my fear
(It was so quiet actually I thought it dead)
And stepped to the sea as lightly as if I had
Wings or were web-footed or had grown a fin-feather.

But the wind finned me and a wave washed off my wing
And the water took to my toes; they were not webby.
I was not amphibian after all but a sinking
Stone—named, indeed, Peter the Rocky.
O all a big lump of suddenly petrified down
With fear awake in my arms, squalling *DROWN.*

MATTHEW ON THE ROUT OF THE TEMPLE

It was not new to me to see them behave
Like money changers, the changers of counterfeit fun
At women who hovered and offered some satisfaction
To the dove dealers, and the doves, and every dove

Calling, they must have all been calling *Love.*
They must have been calling *Love* or they must have
    done
Its fluttering. Or they may have done none.
I don't know no I don't know what to believe.

He had said, *Have faith as the mustard-seed symbol,*
And, *For the laden, baptismal rest by the sea,*
And, *Where two are together with me, I'm the light.*
Those were the awes He pointed to, to tremble
Us, not a house built by the sand-handed me
Where He was a man for a minute—and ready to fight.

JUDAS

A king cannot have a carpenter after his throne.
Every patriot knows where his duty lies.
And if there is silver to seal the bargain, the price
Is nothing; it speaks to soldiers in a tongue known.

What kind of a state, what kind of an honored crown
With no visible head? What kind of a man eyes
A commoner at his miracles and turns and denies
Country to let such swindle long go on?

I told them I'd do it. I told them to give me the money.
I told them to watch, for I would deliver a kiss.
We're almost on him. . . . He said, *What you do, do
    quickly;*
Now I cannot remember the reasons that led me to
    this.
I have my own volcano active in me
But I will stop it, sire, to a civic hiss.

SAUL

When I set out from Jerusalem that day
I had high-priest permission to rope for the lair
More prophets of falseness, and I started sure
I worked for the cause of the genuine Jehovah.
I knew what they said of me—not a heart but a
Makeshift. I had a heart all right; what's more:
I was just as conscientious in my fire
As any who looked at me and, dry-mouthed, away.

Stone in the brilliance: *Saul, why persecute me?*
Was it Stephen's or the voice of another martyr
Shocking me out of Damascus to a better name?
Conversion is watching your highflying beliefs as they
Go sss-T! and you spend your life at an altar
Howling to the One hit you had not aimed at Him.

STORY-BOOK SONNETS

FLOOD

By the Pied Piper, him of Hamlin, were the rats
Enticed to teary death, and by a music
They had not known enough to belittle the like.
(O they'd have said cacophony was *Cats!*)
They never dreamed destruction or whatever waits
Under the water for a sort of embryonic
Return from land; and who would ever suspect
Piping could be perilous sharps and flats?

We were that way about water too:
We didn't know it was there but squeaked and followed
The lively lay of what our earth could do
And a great roar rose! but we were not awed.
Stand still and swallow now as we go down
The music that is sweet by which we drown.

BLUEBEARD HOUSE

He said: "Take a door and open it
And by my beard that's blue love too shall enter
All all of them all—but only one; remember
Turn from the knob it is not best to need.

"This house has held me long, and the wives—I regret
They were many, but you are the tree of the timber
Will make this mansion proud again at your
Obedient shade; and the others I shall forget."

He said it, and I have learned ears and I ought to listen
And leave this door (like death, intriguing) shut;
But it is a part of a house I am not yet in,
It is a part of a proof that he opens not.
I turn this key as symbol of a heart
That will not have a passion with a locked part.

DECLARATION

If I had a magic carpet and could go
Into the tall trees and even above
To see what mountain tops are molded of,
I would not leave you, Love. Never! No!

Who would wish to sail off in the garrulous glow
To silence? The look of a city light might have
Strange significance if seen from far enough
But who would wish it? I would not have it so.

Rather than ride resplendent in the breeze,
My red cloak billowing like beautiful wings
That waft (personally, where no plane sees)
Eagles and all wonderfully flying things
—Rather than ride thus greatly but go
Without you, no. I'd hardly have it so.

NON-SONNETS

TROUBLE IN TENNESSEE

We know that a tremendous Tennessee flurry
Of flakes in the air does not mean the story
Has to end happily in a white morning.
We have slept hopefully and waked to no adorning.

We have been slow in syllable, had our hillbillies,
Laughed in the movies at our own willy-nillies,
And believed still that there is something in gesture,
Something in slowness, something no rush to endure.

We have motored north of the Mason-Dixon,
Have been known to brake a little at the line
Where the heart is a slave-owner, damnrebel,
And cottons to picked loving by the bale.

144999

LIKE HER LOOKING BACK

Like her looking back at a fast-going town
  To see: Is it down?
You turn: Is a certain flame still there?
  And feel a flare.

Difficult to douse. Go about it slowly,
  Into it wholly.
On a pillar of salt let waters run
  To spill a solution.

FOR JONATHAN, NO SONG

The magnificent things you might have said!
    You thought them often enough—
Commendations like ours of the Lord and the dead
    And O loverish fluff.

Easy to praise God or the angelically distant
    Who seem unpained at noise,
Or the lover to whom no note is discordant
    That the marvelous throat employs.

No, the compliment had to be in hush
    —Touche' to a tasteful ear—
Honoring modesty of the flesh
    Even at an earned air.

"AUNT JUANNE MAY NOT LAST THE NIGHT"

Happily polishing their harps today,
    Bragging of songs just done,
Trying their halos in a new jaunty way:
    Already she's perking up heaven

Though she breathes heavily in oxygen here,
    Gaiety tented down.
She is not herself any longer in air
    Blanketing the sun.

As for us, O alone if she should go
    Journeying to Hereafter
But I'd love to slip in on the party they'll throw
    And sip the delicious laughter.

AERIAL LESSON

After a squall boding and bringing ill
We welcomed the unfluttered feeling of air that stayed
    still
And said it would suit us if never again the hand
Over wind and heart stirred more than bare being's
    demand.

We had not figured on getting what we desired
Or else we might have remembered that the storm was
    sired
By monotony such as we turned our backs to assure
Each other we wanted—nearly breathless composure.

But we are learning. The quiet begins to speak:
Would you be embalmed in a calm? Awake. Now,
    awake.
And we smile at old ignorance, glad that at least we
    know
Intelligence when we feel it in the enlivened blow.

MIDAS

Because I told him I reckoned
His music sounded second,
Apollo said, "It appears
Midas has asses' ears."

Terrible to discover
You must keep under cover
—Or the part that enjoys jeers:
Midas has asses' ears!

But only the barber knows
What under the turban grows.
He sees, sharp as his shears,
That Midas has asses' ears

And passes his little learning
On to the earth, discerning
Himself of the commoners:
King Midas has asses' ears.

You cannot give to the dust
And leave silence in trust.
The reed rises up and whispers,
"Midas has asses' ears."

Critic, have your opinion
But think of the sun's dominion.
You may be a me, with my hearers:
Midas has asses' ears.

COOK

I'll remember the day till I am done.
    In the yard, right after rain,
I mused at the mixing (no apron on!)
    And made me a mud-pie man.

Then I had to fly, for the big-size bear
    Came grumbling back for me.
His eyes at the window! O everywhere
    He wept, "Where is she?"

When he lumbered on I ran to find
    Mine that I had molded . . .
Old dirty water! I stomped in it and
    Lifted a fist and scolded.

I'M SICK, EVERYBODY

"I'm sick, everybody! Everybody, I'm sick!"
Looking out at the call of a neighbor tot,
I saw as she added a sturdy kick
To heated singing about her lot.

I suppose her stomach had acted up;
Certainly the throat spoke nothing wrong
But Mercury in her had taken a leap
And perhaps fever inspired the song.

Today I can sympathize with those
Too sick for a neighbor sight at the middle
Still most alive till the dance halls close
When a midnight meaning has got them ill.

I'm sick, everybody. Everybody, I'm sick.
My Mercury moves in an old goat way
And butts at grace, is a little tragic,
And the fire is up on a fevered play.